Freelancing

How to Make Money Freelancing and Build an Entire Career Online

by **K.C. McAllister**

Table of Contents

Introduction

Not that long ago, people couldn't have imagined being able to work from home. Who would have thought it possible to fully perform a job and make money using your computer, working whenever and wherever you want? It sounds a little too good to be true, right? Well it's not. Not at all, in fact. Today we're living in a different era. Many people are using their knowledge, skill, and experience to make a really nice living, working from home (or the park, or the beach – who knows where they actually are???). There have even been numerous computer software and internet platforms built for those who want to become online freelancers. Hundreds of Thousands of jobs are available for an online freelancer!

Now, when you think about that number, it looks pretty attractive and may make you believe it's relatively easy to get freelance work. But it isn't necessarily so easy. *Why Not?* Well that number merely demonstrates the demand for freelancers, but not the supply. There over 15 million freelancers nowadays. So how can you thrive as an online freelancer, and be sure that you can get busy and stay busy? That's what this book is going to help you with. The purpose of this book is to help you optimize your profile, improve your skills and knowledge in order to become better than most of the other freelancers, establish a good reputation to get repeat business, all of which will result in a solid and profitable career as freelancer.

Of course, I can't guarantee you'll make a certain amount of money in any specific period of time, but I can definitely help get you on the right track to being one step ahead of the game, thus increasing your chance of getting work.

Chapter 1: Optimize Your Profile

The first step is creating an account on one (or several) of the common Freelancing websites (such as oDesk, Elance, Freelancer, Guru, iFreelance, etc.). Of course, this involves the simple task of filling out the usual information such as name, e-mail and password. However, this is already where most freelancers make Mistake #1. Lots of people signing up to be online freelancers have read success stories about those who have made a lot of money this way, and now they can't wait to become one themselves. So, they jump online, create an account, and start searching for a job right away. This over-simplification and over-eagerness is dangerous.

What you need is a profile that will stand out by shouting (figuratively) *"Hey, I'm the right person for the specific job you are offering!"* How do you build this kind of profile? This chapter includes a lot of information that will help you optimize your profile to secure work faster.

Basic Information – Be Truthful and Thorough

First of all, you need to fill in the information about you. Present yourself as you are. Do not add any information that's not true. You should provide information about your education, and also any certifications, licensing, or other recognition, diplomas, etc. you've received. Also include all of the jobs you're had over the past year, at a minimum, and upload at least one project as part of your portfolio. Because Clients sometimes are skeptical at first, they don't always trust what they read in your description, so the portfolio is there to speak for itself, attesting to your skills and knowledge. If you are hoping to get work as a freelance Writer, for example, upload some writing samples. If you're hoping to get work as a graphic designer or logo designer, of course upload some samples of your graphic design projects.

The Importance of Taking the Tests

The next step is to take as many tests available that are relevant to your field.

- If you are a writer, then things like spelling, grammar, English, and vocabulary tests are a must. The test for Microsoft Word is also recommended, as you will be using that software the most.

- If you are Computer Programmer, then take all tests available that will prove your knowledge in the programming language you know, and also about general programming.

- If you are into Finance and Accounting, you'll need to take the Accounting principles test, as well as the QuickBooks (or whichever software you use for that purpose) test.

- If you want to be an Assistant (often called "Virtual Assistant" since you're not physically present), then you'll need office skills, which you can prove by taking Office Skills test, Virtual Assistant test, and some of the Microsoft Office tests.

Figure out which niche you want to specialize in, then search for the relevant and related tests that your Clients may deem to be important, and do your very best. Potential Clients do look at these scores, and if they're comparing two potential Freelancers, whose profiles otherwise look equivalent, your score (or the fact that you've taken the tests at all) could be the deciding factor.

The Written Description – Be Specific

The last part of your profile is the written description. Here, you'll want to speak of things such as your reliability, communication skills, and positive attitude (or whatever personality or character traits you possess that may be valuable to someone you may work with). Also, it's a really good idea to include a list of all the services you can provide, called "Areas of Expertise", in bullet-point format beneath your general paragraph-format description. This list is one of the most important parts of optimizing your profile. Most employers or Clients are looking for a Specialist for a certain task. They want someone who has specific knowledge in a specific area. For example, instead of listing "Social Media," you should break it down into all the Social Media platforms you are capable of working on (ex: Facebook, Twitter, Pinterest, etc.). Or as another example, if you are capable of creating a website, don't just list "website development," but instead explain the exact platforms you are capable of using, such as "HTML Website Coding" or "CSS Website Coding," etc. That way, if a Client knows specifically that he or she wants to find a Freelancer to build an HTML website, they may search for "HTML", and come across your profile before they find someone else whose simply says, "Website Development". And even if they do find the other profile, then they'll have to go to the trouble of sending the Freelancer a message, asking whether or not they're capable of writing in HTML.

See where I'm heading? You can make the Client's choice (to hire YOU) much easier by being specific. By being specific, you've already eliminated a big chunk of your competition.

If you feel you're missing certain skills, you can always learn them later on, as you do more and more freelancing work, and then add them to your profile. Your profile shouldn't be something that you just create once, and then leave it alone for months and months. Rather, you should be updating it regularly, and adding to it, especially as you develop more experience and skills.

Think Like a Client / Employer

The key really is to think like a Client as you're creating your own profile. Would you consider hiring yourself? What could make your profile stand out even more? What else might that employer or Client be looking for that's missing?

The specific keywords in your profile are critical. Ask yourself this question: What keywords might my potential employer or Client input into his or her search box when looking for me? Use the answers to this question in creating your bullet-point list. For example, you shouldn't list *"I am good at writing."*

11

Think about it. There is absolutely no way that a Client would search for you by typing in *"I am good at writing."* Rather, he or she may input something like *"creative writing"* or *"technical writing"* or *"blog post writing,"* you get the idea. And if you do all three of these, then by all means – include all three in your list!

Chapter 2: Profile No-No's

Now that you know what you should include in your profile, here's a list of things NOT to include, if you're hoping to attract employers and clients.

- Do not write a lot of background information about yourself. Nobody wants to waste 15 minutes reading your personal or professional history. Remember, these Clients may be comparing dozens of Freelancers for the position – they are browsing through profiles quickly, so you'll want them to pick up on the highlights of what you have to offer with just a glance. They can't do this if it's buried in long paragraphs. Also, actions (or examples in this case) are better than words, so let your portfolio speak for you. Make sure your text can be read within +/- 3 minutes, and that it's organized with nice structure. Don't just input information as you think of it. Instead, open a Word document, write everything you think may be important and valuable, and then edit it carefully into a short text where every word counts, and so that the Clients will finish reading it with a full understanding of what kind of a person you are and the skills you have to offer.

- Do not beg for job. If you start begging that shows that you are not a good employee, because people beg only when they can't find a job or if they feel they're not good enough for the job. Be professional (and confident) at all times, even if you're in dire need of a job.

- Do not write long cover letters. Again, nobody wants to waste more than a couple minutes reading what you offer. Always write a short and clear cover letter, and BE SURE to directly answer the questions the Client has requested you to address in the cover letter. This lets the Client know that you can listen and follow instructions carefully.

- Do not apply for jobs that you are not sure you can do. You don't want to embarrass yourself, and earn a bad rating on your profile. If you don't know how to do something, that's what Chapter 4 is about.

- Do not apply for more jobs than you can handle. This is Mistake #2 made by many freelancers. If you have a job that takes most of your time, do not apply for more. This is just bad business and will hurt your reputation. You may delay one or the other project, make someone wait too long, or worse, miss the deadline. This is another way to get a bad rating on your profile.

Beware of the Rating System

As alluded to earlier, keep in mind these freelancing websites have rating systems, whereby a Client or Employer you've done work with has the ability to rate you, your skills, your level of service, the work you did for them, your communication ability, your promptness, etc. When you get a bad rating, or several bad ratings, it's like a big red flag to other potential Clients that says "DON'T WORK WITH ME. I'M UNRELIABLE AND PREVIOUS CLIENTS HAVE NOT BEEN HAPPY WITH MY WORK." It will be extremely difficult to get more work after this. Whereas, on the other hand, if you keep your Clients very happy and satisfy their requests, do a good job, and communicate well, then you are likely to get a 5-star review. This says to other potential Clients "I AM RELIABLE, A HARD WORKER, A GOOD COMMUNICATOR, ALWAYS DO A GREAT JOB, AND PREVIOUS CLIENTS HAVE BEEN EXTREMELY SATISFIED WITH MY WORK." Well in this case, believe me, your workload as a freelancer has the potential to grow exponentially!

The rating system can either be your friend, or your foe. I suggest making it your friend.

Chapter 3: Learn Your Way to Success

You should know by now that there are many freelancers like you. It does not matter what you offer, there is always someone else who offers that too, and is better at it than you are. In order to become successful, you need to learn from those who already are. Of course, you can't talk to them directly and ask for advice, but you can search for successful freelancers in your area and see what their profile looks like. Check to see if they offer something you don't, for example something that you also offer but forgot to include on your list. You can take a look at their previous jobs and see what they did, and how they earned for it. If you don't know how to do that yet, LEARN. You will read a bit more about this in Chapter 7 which will remind you again that learning and improving yourself is crucial in order to increase your value on the freelancer market.

eLearn: eLearning simply means learning things online. In today's computer age, you can learn just about anything online. And you should be doing this regularly to develop and improve your skills and knowledge base. This will make you so much more competitive. Check to see what other successful freelancers in your field know, and make a list of everything you need to learn. From there, search online for websites about those topics, or YouTube guides, Wiki-how-to guides, and even books or workbooks online. It doesn't matter how you learn, but it's critical that you find a way to constantly increase your knowledge, improve your skill set, and then update your profile accordingly.

Create Goals: And I don't mean things like "I want to make $1000 in one week". I am talking about goals for learning, including deadlines, for example "I will be able to offer the [a specific service] by September 9th of this year." Have a goal to become better than the top freelancers in your field. If you want to build an entire career as an online freelancer and make a lot of money, then you'll need to constantly set these big goals for yourself. Set a goal that looks unreal or unachievable, and then do all you can to reach it. You will see the difference within a month or two, and your confidence will increase too!

Chapter 4: Every Beginning Is Hard

As the chapter title says, every beginning is hard. As a new freelancer, you're starting off with NO feedback on your profile, and it's common knowledge that clients and employers usually prefer to work with freelancers with proven experience in their field.

This is the point where a lot of freelancers, who aren't getting work right away, become disappointed, give up, and quit. Most Clients and Employers simply skip over the profiles without work experience, and therefore the only way to convince him that you are the right person for the job is through your cover letter. Now, from the first chapter you already know that your cover letter should not be long. But because this may be the only way to leave a good impression as you're starting off, you'll need to craft your cover letter carefully, even before you start applying for jobs. This is especially important for new freelancers with no rating at all.

How to write a great cover letter:

You should put yourself in the shoes of the person looking for a freelancer. What kind of cover letter would you like to read from the perfect freelancer? You need to be honest, and you should mean everything you say. If you think you do not have enough experience, mention it, and go on to explain that you're hoping to gain more experience and you're willing to learn as you go. But again, be reminded that if you don't think you can fulfill the requirements of the job, then DO NOT APPLY. If you fail for any reason, you risk getting a bad rating.

As a new freelancer, you want to concentrate first on completing a few jobs that will increase your rating and prove to future employers that you are capable of working and you can meet deadlines. Good ratings and an optimized profile will bring you many invitations for interviews. Yes, employers will often ask to interview you for a certain job. But before all that, you need to complete as many short-term, boring jobs, and even low-paying jobs as possible. The first month is the hardest, and you should now that even those freelancers now earning over $5,000 dollars per month, were likely once data typing for $2 per hour.

Mistake #3 that usually leads to not getting any work, is applying for big projects without having any feedback or ratings at all. Remember, you are competing with at least a dozen other freelancers that have proven themselves in that field, so don't expect to get employed there. As mentioned above, you need to focus on completing short-term, boring, low-paying jobs at first. Do data entry typing, or really you can do anything that will earn you good 5-star feedback on your profile. Again, your goal in the first month is to get as much good feedback as you can.

Mistake #4 is being afraid to ask your Client for clarification, instead proceeding to do something that you are not sure about. It does not matter if you are a new freelancer, or you have experience with many previous jobs. Before you get started, you need to make sure you know exactly what you are supposed to be doing. NEVER be afraid to ask if you aren't sure about something. It is not shameful to ask, but it is shameful not to know. It is better to ask for more information than work on a project and provide a bad end-product. Again, this will result in a poor rating.

But the absolute worst mistake you can make is Mistake #5: Give up. Every beginning is hard, but you need to sacrifice some time in the beginning to build a great profile and get some good reviews if you really want to ultimately build an entire career as an online freelancer. As mentioned above, even the most successful freelancers were once working for $2 per hour, if not less. This is just part of the whole process that unfortunately you can't skip. But once you get past it, you will be able to apply for much better jobs that will increase your experience and give you more money than you thought at the beginning. Remember, as a professional freelancer, you will get to choose where you work, the time you work, and the amount of work you do each day. Whenever you feel like giving up, remind yourself of all the benefits!

Chapter 5: Get Software

Up until the point of having a few solid 5-star reviews, it didn't matter what kind of skills and knowledge you have because these short-term, easy, and boring jobs usually just require a computer and internet connection.

But now that this phase is over with, and you have a great profile with excellent reviews, you're ready to move up in the world in freelancing. It's time for you to give yourself your first raise!

You'll also need to identify and be sure that your profile is clear about what field you're choosing to specialize in. Choose a field you're both interested in, and somewhat skilled at. This will make your work as a freelancer more enjoyable. And be sure to be specific. Clients are looking for specific work to be completed, with specific requirements, and therefore will usually look for freelancers with a specific specialty so they can get the best person for the job. Again, your goal should be to become the best freelancer in your chosen specific field.

Of course, it's fine to be "second best" or even "really good." But for now, let's stick with the goal to become "one of the best" freelancers in your chosen field. How can you do this? Well, as mentioned earlier, constant and continuous learning cannot be over-emphasized in this whole process. But also, a very important factor may be the software you're using. If you want to build a career as an online freelancer, then depending on your field, you may have to invest some money to buy the best software available for your type of work. This will not only improve your performance, but it will help you be competitive. Also, you can list your expertise of this software in your profile. Remember, you are trying to beat out other freelancers in the same field. How will you compete with a graphic designer who is using the latest version of Photoshop if you're only using a free online software program instead?

No matter what your chosen field is, there is likely a software program that will help you become better and more proficient. There's transcribing software, analysis software, forecasting software, accounting software, designer software, copyscape software, etc. Instead of thinking of these software programs as costing you money, you should actually think of them costing you money if you don't purchase them. With the software, you can show to a potential Client how you're invested in your field, you're knowledgeable and up to date with the latest tools, and you're simply prepared and ready to go to work. It may seem like just a small advantage, but it's these small advantages that make the difference in you getting hired rather than a competitor. If you need to use a certain software program but don't know how, again, go back to the chapter where I discussed eLearning. There are guides and videos for just about everything these days. You really have no excuse.

Chapter 6: Building a Good Reputation

If you want a career as freelancer, then you need a good reputation. You need to be recognized among other freelancers to get each job, then you need to leave a good impression as you're ending each job. How can you do this? Here is a very short list that will help you to build a solid reputation as a competent, efficient, and hard-working freelancer.

1. Always do your best. Mistake #6 is that many freelancers just do the work as quickly as possible, so they can earn fast money. Focus on quality. Of course, it's important to meet the deadline, but it is equally as important to deliver quality work. If you feel you are not able to finish the project by the deadline, you need to let your employer know as soon as possible. If you tell them early, they'll be much more understanding than if you tell them at the time of the deadline. By then, they may be angry that you didn't let them know sooner.

2. Be honest. Always be honest. If you are honest and you inform the Client or

Employer of everything that's happening, you will earn his or her respect. And that will help you to develop a good working relationship, which is explained below.

3. Build good relationships with those you work with. If you do your best, if you are honest and you send notification to him or her regarding the project, you will earn trust and respect, which is the foundation for a good working relationship with that person. Regardless if you are a new freelancer or not, you should try to build as many relationships like this one as possible. Remember, this is where your money will come from. If you leave a good impression, there is a very high chance that the same person will ask you to work for him again, and again, and again. As the 80/20 rule goes, you will get 80% results from 20% of the things you do. It's the same here. About 80% of the money you will earn will come from 20% of the people you work with. However, do not focus on those 20% only. Build good relationships with everyone. You never know what will happen next, or where your next job will come from.

4. Do not chase money. If you focus on making money you will never make any. If you focus on becoming a better freelancer in your specific field, and offer top class service, then the money will follow and you will build the reputation you want.

As mentioned above, once you've completed enough work, and received great feedback with high ratings, there will be employers asking you to work for them. You'll be well on your way to being a successful freelancer with a great reputation within just a few months.

Chapter 7: Keep Learning (Yes, MORE Learning)

This chapter is simply a reminder of what I mentioned in Chapter 3, about how important continual learning is to this process.

If you want to have an amazingly successful career as a freelancer, you need to sacrifice your time at the beginning. As mentioned previously, you can easily benchmark your skills and knowledge against those of the best freelancers in your field. You can easily find out what is paying off for them, and then focus on learning the same. The number of people learning through the internet is increasing and all you need to do is figure out what exactly it is that you need to learn. The more knowledge you acquire is what allows you to apply for more jobs. The more jobs you can apply to, the higher chance you have to win a project, and the project of your choosing at that! Use all eLearning platforms that offer courses of what you want to learn. Use whatever method of learning you can find, or you prefer, but always make it a goal to improve as much as possible.

In order to earn more money, you need to invest time in improving yourself. The best way to do that is to learn every single day. If you think that's too hard, then you need to start considering the alternatives (going back to a traditional office job, moving back in with your parents to save money, etc). The first month is going to be difficult. Just accept that as a fact. But as you develop goals, and create a routine of learning and improving, you'll develop an excitement for your new knowledge, and an eagerness to utilize it on a project. This will constantly be a motivating factor to improve your profile and apply for more work.

So, start by setting aside 1-2 hours a day to simply study and develop new skills. After 2 weeks, you won't see this as something hard to do, but as something you actually enjoy doing. This time investment and effort will eventually pay off big-time, by increasing your value on the freelance market, and help you to build a career as an online freelancer.

Just get through the beginning, and you'll soon reap all the benefits of a successful online freelancer.

Conclusion

As you can see, building a career as online freelancer may be slightly more complicated that it originally sounds, especially in the beginning. The fact that there are so many online jobs available does not mean that it is easy to get one. However, this guide should help you start making money as an online freelancer within 30 days. And if you follow it closely, you will have a well-crafted profile that will attract clients and employers looking for good freelancers. Optimize your profile, start working on short-term lower paying jobs, and earn some 5-star reviews. Choose your field of specialty, get the right software, keep learning continuously, and you will soon see the difference, and the dollars.

Last, you can rest assured that there are plenty of people who work from home, and earn more money than you'd expect, and more money than those who travel to the office each day to work at a desk from 9 to 5. If you dedicate yourself to this process, get through the beginning rough patch, and focus on improving yourself continuously, you can earn a living this way too. Be patient, and don't give up. You can do it – why not? The benefits are enormous. You'll be able to work from wherever, whenever, and with whomever. If this sounds appealing, why not get started right now?

I hope you found this guide tremendously useful. If you did, please take a moment and leave a nice review for it on Amazon – I'd really appreciate it! Thank you, and good luck!

Made in the USA
Coppell, TX
14 February 2024

29004260R00030